Logos of
America's Largest Companies

David E. Carter
Editor

Distributed by 1033 La Posada Drive, Suite 250
Austin, Texas 78752
HOOVERS Main: (800) 486-8666
BUSINESS PRESS Fax: (512) 374-4501

Art Direction Book Co.
10 E. 39th Street
New York, NY 10016

©Copyright, 1988 Art Direction Book Co.

ISBN 0-88108-059-4
LCCC#: 88-071637

Printed in Japan.

This book was produced due to the requests of many people who wanted a book that showed "what the big companies' logos look like."

A list of roughly 900 companies was compiled from various business directories. Each of those firms was sent a letter requesting a logo to be included in this book.

The following pages include some 600 designs representing a good cross-section of the logos of America's largest companies.

Harvey Hubbell, Incorporated
Orange, CT

Leggett & Platt, Incorporated
Carthage, MO

Tyson Foods, Incorporated
Springdale, AR

Ryder System, Inc.
Miami, FL

RYDER SYSTEM INC

Potomac Electric Power Company
Washington, DC

FMC Corporation
Chicago, IL

K-Mart Corporation
Troy, MI

H.H. Robertson Company
Pittsburgh, PA

Cooper Companies
Akron, OH

Green Tree Acceptance, Inc.
St. Paul, MN

Western Digital Corp.
Irvine, CA

San Diego Gas & Electric
San Diego, CA

Owens/Corning Fiberglas
Toledo, OH

Jim Walter Corporation
Tampa, FL

Whirlpool Corporation,
Benton Harbor, MI

PACIFIC POWER

Pacific Telesis Center
San Francisco, CA

Echlin Corporate Headquarters
Branford, CT

ECHLIN

Deere & Company
Moline, IL

Deere & Company
Moline, IL

Super Valu Stores, Inc.
Minneapolis, MN

Washington Gas Light Company
Washington, DC

Washington
Gas

Trans World Airlines, Inc.
New York, NY

13

American Home Products Corp.
New York, NY

USX Corporation
Pittsburgh, PA

TCBY Systems, Inc.
Little Rock, AR

Minnesota Power
Duluth, MN

Cincinnati Bell, Inc.
Cincinnati, OH

Gerber Products Company
Fremont, MI

Kenner Parker Toys
Parker Brothers
Beverly, MA

RJR Nabisco
Atlanta, GA

LIQUID AIR CORPORATION
INDUSTRIAL GASES DIVISION

Primark Corporation
McLean, VA

Wendy's International, Incorporated
Dublin, OH

Measurex Corporation
Cupertino, CA

Colt Industries, Inc.
New York, NY

Colt Industries

Tandem Computers, Inc.
Cupertino, CA

US West, Inc.
Englewood, CO

Georgia-Pacific
Atlanta, GA

Signet Bank/Virginia
Richmond, VA

SIGNET®

Signet Banking Corporation

First National Bank of Maryland
Baltimore, MD

First National
Bank
of Maryland

The Hartford Steam Boiler
Inspection and Insurance Co.
Hartford, CT

Ryan's Family Steak House, Inc.
Greer, SC

Land's End, Inc.
Dodgeville, WI

Montana Power Company
Butte, MT

The Pittston Company
Greenwich, CT

Mitchell Energy & Development Corp.
The Woodlands, TX

US Air
Washington D.C.

Hannaford Brothers Company
Portland, ME

Pennsylvania Power & Light Company
Allentown, PA

Boston Edison
Boston, MA

Chrysler Corporation
Highland Park, MI

Central Soya
Fort Wayne, IN

Grumman Corporation
Bethpage, NY

AMGen
Thousand Oaks, CA

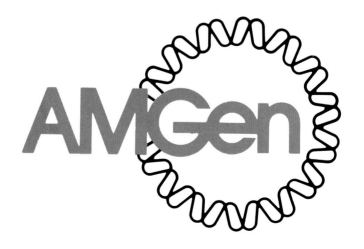

24

Equitable Gas
Pittsburgh, PA

STANADYNE
Windsor, CT

STANADYNE

ALLTEL Corporation
Hudson, OH

HON Industries
Muscatine, IA

HON Industries
Muscatine, IA

CORRYHIEBERT

HON Industries
Muscatine, IA

HON Industries
Muscatine, IA

26

Pall Corporation
East Hills, NY

Dynatech Corporation
Burlington, MA

National Cooperative Refinery Assn.
McPherson, KS

Becton Dickinson and Company
Franklin Lakes, NJ

BAIRNCO Corporation
New York, NY

BAIRNCO Corporation
New York, NY

BAIRNCO Corporation
New York, NY

Sovran Bank
Richmond, VA

CF Industries, Inc.
Long Grove, IL

CF Industries, Inc.
Long Grove, IL

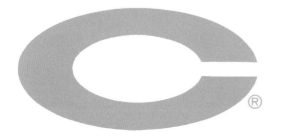

ASARCO, Incorporated
New York, NY

ASARCO

General Dynamics
St. Louis, MO

GENERAL DYNAMICS

Hercules, Incorporated
Wilmington, DE

Hoechst Celanese Corporation
Somerville, NJ

Intel Corporation
Santa Clara, CA

First Wisconsin National Bank
Milwaukee, WI

FIRST WISCONSIN
MILWAUKEE

International Technology Corporation
Monroeville, PA

INTERNATIONAL
TECHNOLOGY
CORPORATION

Raytheon Company
Lexington, MA

**First Interstate Bancorp,
Los Angeles, CA**

**AVERY Corporate Center
Pasadena, CA**

**DANA Corporate Offices
Toledo, OH**

American Electric Power
Columbus, OH

Rexnord, Incorporated
Brookfield, WI

IU International
Philadelphia, PA

Texaco, Inc.
White Plains, NY

Contel Corporation
Atlanta, GA

Triangle Industries, Inc.
New York, NY

LSI Logic Corporation
Milpitas, CA

Russell Corporation
Alexander City, AL

Fina Oil and Chemical Company
Dallas, TX

**Witco Corporation
New York, NY**

Witco

**Eastman Kodak Company
Rochester, NY**

**The Boeing Company
Seattle, WA**

American Airlines
DFW Airport, TX

Reichhold
White Plains, NY

REICHHOLD

General Electric
Fairfield, CT

Fleming Companies, Inc.
Oklahoma City, OK

Fleming
Companies, Inc.

Media General
Richmond, VA

BASF Corporation
Parsippany, NJ

BASF

EG&G Incorporated
Wellesley, MA

Ashton-Tate
Torrance, CA

Sterling Drug, Inc.
New York, NY

STERLING DRUG INC.

Foster Wheeler Corporation
Clinton, NJ

Robertshaw Controls Company
Richmond, VA

Automatic Data Processing, Inc.
Roseland, NJ

North American Philips Corp.
New York, NY

North American Philips Corporation

Thomas J. Lipton, Inc.
Englewood Cliffs, NJ

The Quaker Oats Company
Chicago, IL

The Singer Company
Stamford, CT

SINGER

UNOCAL
Los Angeles, CA

Maxus Energy Corporation
Dallas, TX

Minnegasco
Minneapolis, MN

Crane Company
New York, NY

Lockheed Corporation
Calabasas, CA

Pfizer, Inc.
New York, NY

Nashua Corp.
Nashua, NH

Nashua

TRINOVA Corp.
Maumee, OH

TRINOVA

General Mills, Inc.
Minneapolis, MN

Navistar International Corp.
Chicago, IL

Navistar International Corp.
Chicago, IL

Ferro Corporation
Cleveland, OH

Alco Standard Corporation
Valley Forge, PA

ALCO Standard Corporation

Schering—Plough
Madison, NJ

Louisiana-Pacific
Portland, OR

National Service Industries, Inc.
Atlanta, GA

Federal-Mogul Corporation
Detroit, MI

Sara Lee Corporation
Chicago, IL

SARA LEE CORPORATION

Fuqua Industries, Inc.
Atlanta, GA

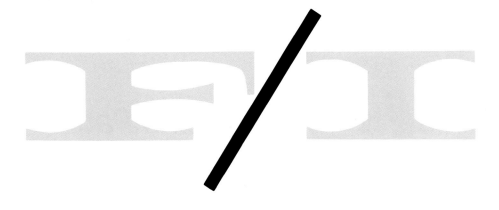

The Pillsbury Company
Minneapolis, MN

Mohasco Corporation
Amsterdam, NY

Hormel
Austin, MN

Chicago and Northwestern Railroad
Chicago, IL

Chicago and Northwestern Railroad
Chicago, IL

Loctite Corporation
Newington, CT

Borden
Columbus, OH

Cincinnati Milacron, Inc.
Cincinnati, OH

CINCINNATI
MILACRON

NORTON Company
Worchester, MA

CBI Industries, Inc.
Oak Brook, IL

Premier Industrial Corp.
Cleveland, OH

Southeast Banking Corp.
Miami, FL

Pacific Gas and Electric Company
San Francisco, CA

Ball Corporation
Muncie, IN

C.R. Bard, Inc.
Murray Hill, NJ

Johnson Controls, Inc.
Milwaukee, WI

Amdahl Corporation
Sunnyvale, CA

Federal Paper Board Company, Inc.
Riegelwood, NC

NCR Corporation
Dayton, OH

Philadelphia Electric Company
Philadelphia, PA

Tracor, Inc.
Austin, TX

Tracor, Inc.

Bob Evans Farms
Columbus, OH

A.T Cross Company
Lincoln, RI

VF Corporation
Wyomissing, PA

Convergent Technologies
San Jose, CA

Convergent

Tambrands Inc.
Lake Success, NY

TAMBRANDS

The Henley Group, Inc.
Hampton, NH

Kansas City Power & Light Company
Kansas City, MO

May Department Stores Company
St. Louis, MO

General Motors Technical Center
Warren, MI

General Motors

National Intergroup, Inc.
Pittsburgh, PA

NATIONAL
Intergroup, Inc.

South Carolina Electric & Gas Company
Columbia, SC

58

Dominion Bankshares Corporation
Roanoke, VA

NCC National City Bank
Cleveland, OH

Jefferson Pilot
Greensboro, NC

**Liberty National
A Torchmark Company
Birmingham, AL**

**Harsco Corporation
Camphill, PA**

**Scott Paper Company
Philadelphia, PA**

SCOTT

Chesebrough Pond's Inc.
Greenwich, CT

Chesebrough Pond's Inc.

Multimedia, Inc.
Greenville, SC

Staley Continental, Inc.
Rolling Meadows, IL

StaleyContinental, Inc.

Great Northern Nekoosa Corp.
Stamford, CT

Bic Corporation
Milford, CT

Penn Bancorp
Oil City, PA

The Copper Companies, Inc.
Menlo Park, CA

Puget Sound Power & Light Company
Bellevue, WA

The Energy Starts Here

Wells Fargo Bank
San Francisco, CA

State Street Bank and Trust Company
Boston, MA

State Street

Georgia Gulf Corporation
Atlanta, GA

Thorn Apple Valley Inc.
Southfield, MI

National Bank of Detroit
Detroit, MI

The Upjohn Company
Kalamazoo, MI

Kroger
Cincinnati, OH

The Sherwin-Williams Company
Cleveland, OH

McKesson Corporation
San Francisco, CA

The Huntington National Bank
Columbus, OH

G. Heileman Brewing Co., Inc.
La Crosse, WI

Murphy Oil U.S.A., Inc.
El Dorado, AZ

Capital Holding Corporation
Louisville, KY

CapitalHolding

Duke Power Company
Charlotte, NC

 **DUKE POWER**

United States Fidelity and Guaranty Co.
Baltimore, MD

USF&G®
INSURANCE

American Motors Corporation
Southfield, MI

American Motors Corporation

Crestar Financial Corporation
Richmond, VA

MidLantic National Bank
Edison, NJ

MIDLANTIC

Wal-Mart
Bentonville, AR

Norwest Corporation
Minneapolis, MN

Aluminum Company of America
Pittsburgh, PA

Maytag Company
Newton, IA

Masco Corporation
Taylor, MI

Firestone
Akron, OH

Dover Corporation
New York, NY

Kansas City Southern Industries, Inc.
Kansas City, MO

KCSI

Kansas City Southern Industries, Inc.

Texas Industries, Inc.
Dallas, TX

Texas Industries, Inc.

Hillenbrand Industries
Batesville, IN

HILLENBRAND INDUSTRIES

Teledyne, Inc.
Los Angeles, CA

Fairchild Industries, Inc.
Chantilly, VA

Luby's Cafeterias, Inc.
San Antonio, TX

Perkin Elmer
Norwalk, CT

Bank South Corporation
Atlanta, GA

Vulcan Materials Company
Birmingham, AL

Tejon Ranch
Lebec, CA

Genesco, Inc.
Nashville, TN

Universal Leaf Tobacco Company
Richmond, VA

Mapco, Inc.
Tulsa, OK

**West Point Pepperell
West Point, GA**

**Champion International Corporation
Stamford, CT**

Burlington Industries, Inc.
Greensboro, NC

Burlington

A.H. Belo Corporation
Dallas, TX

A.H.BELO
CORPORATION

Lever Brother Company, Inc.
New York, NY

Raychem Corporation
Menlo Park, CA

Raychem

Campbell Soup Company
Camden, NJ

Campbell's® Soups

Union Texas Petroleum
Houston, TX

 **Union Texas Petroleum**

NORTHROP
Los Angeles, CA

NORTHROP

Circus Circus Enterprises, Inc.
Las Vegas, NV

Consolidated Papers, Inc.
Wisconsin Rapids, WI

CONSOLIDATED PAPERS, INC.

Kimberly-Clark
Dallas, TX

Reliance Group Holdings
New York, NY

H.J. Heinz Company
Pittsburgh, PA

SNET
New Haven, CT

The Pullman Company
Princeton, NJ

Harte-Hanks Communications, Inc.
San Antonio, TX

Morton Thiokol, Inc.
Chicago, IL

MORTON THIOKOL, INC.

Pepsico
Purchase, NY

Colgate-Palmolive Company
New York, NY

American Cyanamid Company
Wayne, NJ

Greyhound
Phoenix, AZ

CitiCorp
New York, NY

First Virginia Banks Inc.
Falls Church, VA

American Greetings
Cleveland, OH

Allegheny International
Pittsburgh, PA

Bankers Trust Company
New York, NY

Nalco Chemical Company
Naperville, IL

Southwestern Public Service Co.
Amarillo, TX

Caterpillar, Inc.
Peoria, IL

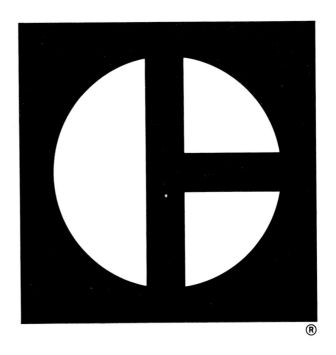

Bethlehem Steel Corporation
Bethlehem, PA

A.H. Robins Company
Richmond, VA

Koppers Company, Inc.
Pittsburgh, PA

KOPPERS

Neutrogena Corporation
Los Angeles, CA

Neutrogena®

The United States Shoe Corp.
Cincinnati, OH

U.S. Shoe

Humana Inc.
Louisville, KY

The Coca-Cola Company
Atlanta, GA

Pacific Resources, Inc.
Honolulu, HI

Pacific Resources, Inc.

Handy & Harman
New York, NY

Worthington Industries, Inc.
Columbus, OH

Rochester Gas and Electric
Rochester, NY

Metro Mobile
New York, NY

Central Illinois
Public Service Company
Springfield, IL

20th Century Insurance Company
Woodland Hills, CA

Owens-Illinois
Toledo, OH

E.I. Du Pont De Nemours & Company
Wilmington, DE

GANNETT Company, Inc.
Washington, DC

Harnischfeger Industries, Inc.
Milwaukee, WI

Harnischfeger Industries, Inc.

Westvaco
New York, NY

Westvāco

Corning Glass Works
Corning, NY

CORNING

Cameron Iron Works, Inc.
Houston, TX

Cameron IRON WORKS, INC.

The Ohio Casualty Insurance Company
Hamilton, OH

United Telecom
Kansas City, MO

Texas Eastern Transmission Corp.
Houston, TX

Detroit Edison
Detroit, MI

Detroit
Edison

A good part of your life.

Standard Register
Dayton, OH

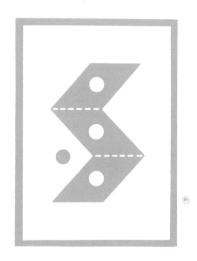

Teradyne, Incorporated
Boston, MA

The Procter & Gamble Company
Cincinnati, OH

Anheuser-Busch Companies
St. Louis, MO

Black & Decker
Towson, MD

First Hawaiian Bank
Honolulu, HI

First Hawaiian Bank

Questar Corporation
Salt Lake City, UT

The Clorox Company
Oakland, CA

Chesapeake
West Point, VA

American Capital Companies
Houston, TX

American Capital®
Capital
MANAGEMENT &
RESEARCH, INC.

Alaska Airlines
Seattle, WA

Alaska Airlines
Fly with a happy face.

GEICO
Washington, DC

GEICO

Barnett Banks, Inc.
Jacksonville, FL

Wertterau Incorporated
Hazelwood, MO

TU Electronics
Dallas, TX

McDonald's Corporation
Oak Brook, IL

United Cable Television
Denver, CO

PSE&G
Newark, NJ

The Walt Disney Company
Burbank, CA

US Healthcare
Bluebell, PA

The Limited, Inc.
Columbus, OH

ECOLAB
Economics Center
St. Paul, MN

United Technologies
Hartford, CT

The Foxboro Company
Foxboro, MA

Pan American World Airways, Inc.
New York, NY

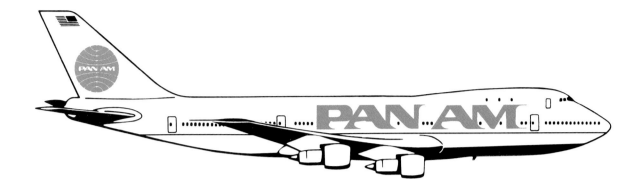

Mid-America Dairymen, Inc.
Springfield, MO

The Citizens and Southern National Bank
Atlanta, GA

Illinois Power Company
Decatur, IL

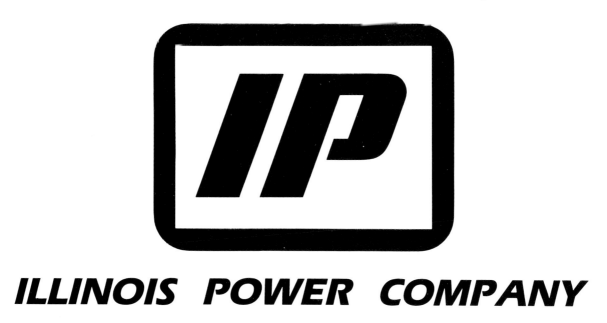

ILLINOIS POWER COMPANY

JC Penney
New York, NY

JCPenney

Puget Sound Bank
Tacoma, WA

Adolph Coors Company
Golden, CO

NL Industries, Inc.
Houston, TX

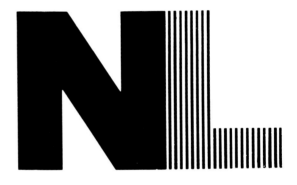

Brockway
Jacksonville, FL

Ashland Oil, Inc.
Ashland, KY

International Business Machines Corp.
White Plains, NY

Santa Fe Southern Pacific Corp.
Chicago, IL

The Gillette Company
Boston, MA

The Gillette Company

Scripps Howard
Cincinnati, OH

SCRIPPS HOWARD

Bolt Beranek and Newman, Inc.
Cambridge, MA

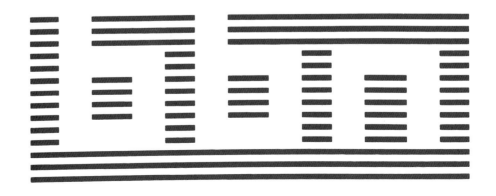

Baker Hughes, Inc.
Houston, TX

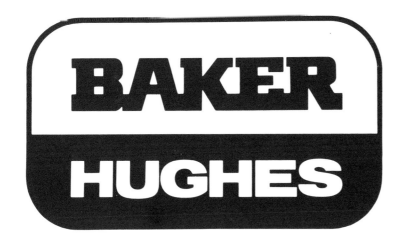

First Chicago Corp.
The First National Bank of Chicago
Chicago, IL

Textron, Inc.
Providence, RI

Hasbro, Inc.
Pawtucket, RI

Hasbro, Inc.
Pawtucket, RI

Westinghouse Electric Corporation
Pittsburgh, PA

SouthTrust Corporation
Birmingham, AL

XIDEX Corporation
Santa Clara, CA

First Tennessee Bank National Assn.
Memphis, TN

FlightSafety International
Flushing, NY

FlightSafety
international
the best safety device in any aircraft is a well trained pilot...

Carter Hawley Hale Stores, Inc.
Los Angeles, CA

First of American Bank Corp.
Kalamazoo, MI

Winn-Dixie Stores, Inc.
Jacksonville, FL

Chemical Waste Mangement, Inc.
Oak Brook, IL

Hecla Mining Company
Coeur d'Alene, ID

GOULD Electronics
Rolling Meadows, IL

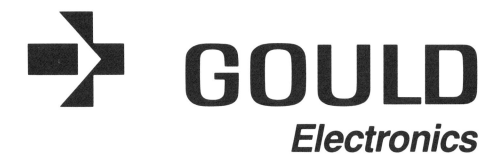

TW Services, Inc.
New York, NY

Public Service Company of Colorado
Denver, CO

ROHR Industries, Inc.
Chula Vista, CA

MDU Resources Group, Inc.
Bismarck, ND

Inland Steel Industries, Inc.
Chicago, IL

Armstrong World Industries, Inc.
Lancaster, PA

Telecredit, Inc.
Los Angeles, CA

Telecredit, Inc.

Portland General Corp.
Portland, OR

Lefkowith, Inc.
Chase Manhattan Bank
New York, NY

The Ryland Group, Inc.
Columbia, MD

Brunswick Corporation
Skokie, IL

Time Incorporated
New York, NY

The Southland Corporation
Dallas, TX

THE SOUTHLAND CORPORATION

Outboard Marine Corp.
Waukegan, IL

Subaru of America
Cherry Hill, NJ

Quaker State Corporation
Oil City, PA

Fifth Third Bank
Cincinnati, OH

Ethyl Corporation
Richmond, VA

Exxon
New York, NY

Sealed Power Corporation
Muskegon, MI

SEALED P⚡WER
A Tradition of Achievement

Dow Jones & Company, Inc.
New York, NY

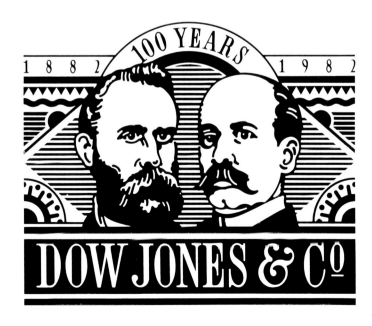

Sonoco Products Company
Hartsville, SC

Wisconsin Power & Light Company
Madison, WI

Wheeling Pittsburgh
Wheeling, WV

Bausch & Lomb
Rochester, NY

Cooper Tire & Rubber Company
Findlay, OH

Zenith Electronics Corporation
Glenview, IL

The Circle K Corporation
Phoenix, AZ

Interstate Brands Corporation
Kansas City, MO

Monsanto
St. Louis, MO

Monsanto

Allied Signal Incorporated
Morristown, NJ

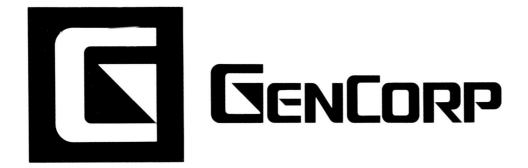

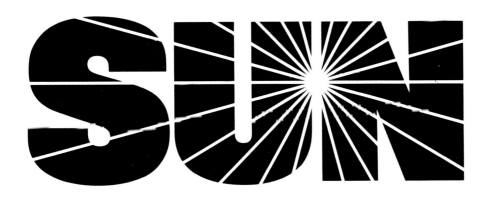

Security Pacific National Bank
Los Angeles, CA

AMP Incorporated
Harrisburg, PA

The Lubrizol Corporation
Wickliffe, OH

Kimball International

Johnson & Johnson
New Brunswick, NJ

Johnson & Johnson

FAMILY OF COMPANIES

Hawaiian Electric Company, Inc.
Honolulu, HI

HEI
Hawaiian Electric Industries, Inc.

CSX Corporation
Richmond, VA

CSX CORPORATION

Farmers Insurance Group of Companies
Los Angeles, CA

**America can depend
on Farmers**

PaineWebber
New York, NY

PaineWebber

Bally Manufacturing Corp.
Chicago, IL

**Molex Incorporated
Lisle, IL**

**Comdisco, Inc.
Rosemont, IL**

**GATX Corportation
Chicago, IL**

MARION Laboratories, Inc.
Kansas City, MO

CG&E The Energy Service Company
Cincinnati, OH

CG&E ■ The Energy
Service
Company

DELUXE Check Printers, Inc.
St. Paul, MN

New York State Electric & Gas Corporation

Good people.
Good service.®

Subsidiary of GM Hughes Electronics

WHERE SMART WORKING WOMEN SAVE 20% TO 50% ON FASHION.

Autodesk, Incorporated
Sausalito, CA

Atlanta Gas Light Company
Atlanta, GA

Kellwood Company
St. Louis, MO

First National Bank of Louisville
Louisville, KY

Tyler Corporation
Dallas, TX

Tyler Corporation

Mellon Bank
Pittsburgh, PA

ACUSON Computed Sonography
Mountain View, CA

Public Service Indiana
Plainfield, IN

PUBLIC SERVICE INDIANA

KAMAN Corporation
Bloomfield, CT

Ingersoll-Rand
Woodcliff Lake, NJ

Sierra Pacific Rsources
Reno, NV

SIERRA PACIFIC RESOURCES

Joseph E. Seagram & Sons, Inc.
New York, NY

KPL Gas Service
Topeka, KS

National Gypsum Company
Dallas, TX

Central Maine Power Company
Augusta, ME

Central Maine Power

Peoples Energy Corporation
Chicago, IL

Peoples Energy Corporation

Allis-Chalmers
Milwaukee, WI

ALLIS-CHALMERS

Hewlett Packard
Palo Alto, CA

HEWLETT PACKARD

Jerrico, Incorporated
Lexington, KY

Jerrico, Incorporated
Lexington, KY

Tektronix
Beaverton, OR

GTE
Stamford, CT

First Pennsylvania Bank N.A.
Philadelphia, PA

Zenith Insurance Company
Van Nuys, CA

Cetus Corporation
Emeryville, CA

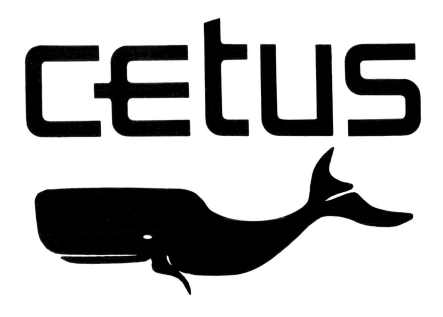

Warner-Lambert Company
Morris Plains, NJ

WARNER
LAMBERT

Maxus Energy Corporation
Dallas, TX

SMS
Malvern, PA

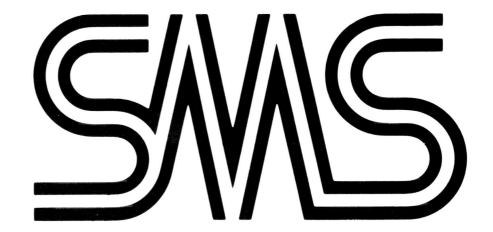

Anchor Glass Container
Tampa, FL

Anchor
Glass Container

SallieMae
Washington, DC

SallieMae

Mattel, Inc.
Hawthorne, CA

York International Corporation
York, PA

Mentor Graphics Corporation
Beaverton, OR

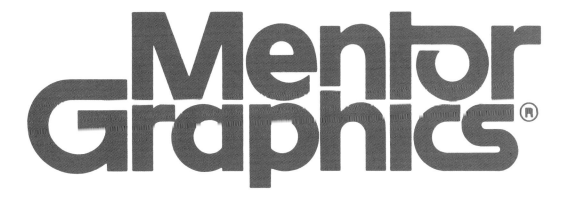

Philip Morris
New York, NY

Great Western Financial Corporation
Beverly Hills, CA

GREAT
WESTERN

GW

Great Western Financial Corporation

Lincoln National
Fort Wayne, IN

Fort Wayne, Indiana 46801

The New York Times Company
New York, NY

Fort Howard Paper Company
Green Bay, WI

Fort Howard

The Coleman Company, Inc.
Wichita, KS

Wisconsin Energy Corporation
Milwaukee, WI

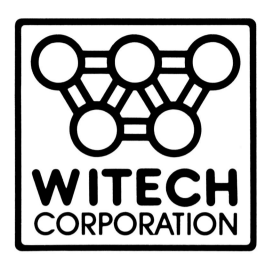

Wisconsin Energy Corporation
Milwaukee, WI

Wisconsin Energy Corporation
Milwaukee, WI

Wisconsin Energy Corporation
Milwaukee, WI

138

Home Federal Savings & Loan Assn.
San Diego, CA

HOME FEDERAL

The Washington Post
Washington, DC

Houghton Mifflin Company
Boston, MA

Houghton Mifflin Company

Louisville Gas & Electric Company
Louisville, KY

Louisville
Gas and Electric
Company

ConAgra, Incorporated
Omaha, NE

Shell Oil Company
Houston, TX

CLECO
Central Louisiana Electric Co., Inc.
Pineville, LA

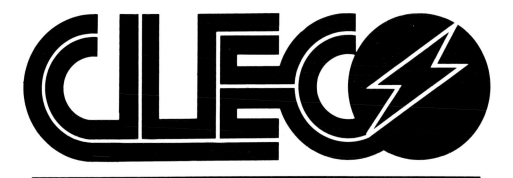

Wilson Foods Corporation
Oklahoma City, OK

HIMONT Incorporated
Wilmington, DE

Alexander & Alexander Services Inc.
New York, NY

Centocor
Malvern, PA

CENTOCOR

Morrison Incorporated
Mobile, AL

MORRISON · INCORPORATED

Safety-Kleen Corporation
Elgin, IL

safety-kleen ®

Lone Star Industries, Inc.
Greenwich, CT

Brown Group, Inc.
St. Louis, MO

Kentucky Utilities Company
Lexington, KY

Great Lakes Chemical Corporation
West Lafayette, IN

Tenneco, Incorporated
Houston, TX

Los Angeles Times
Los Angeles, CA

Dennison
Framingham, MA

Houston Industries, Incorporated
Houston, TX

Katy Industries, Inc.
Elgin, IL

Champion Spark Plug Company
Toledo, OH

Harris Corporation
Melbourne, FL

Carlisle Companies, Incorporated
Cincinnati, OH

Herman Miller Inc.
Zeeland, MI

herman miller

Freeport McMoRan Inc.
New Orleans, LA

Kaiser Aluminum & Chemical Corp.
Oakland, CA

Square D Company
Palatine, IL

Atlantic Richfield Company
Los Angeles, CA

Ford Motor Company
Dearborn, MI

The Chubb Corporation
Warren, NJ

Anadarko Petroleum Corporation
Houston, TX

Helmerich & Payne, Inc.
Tulsa, OK

Moore McCormack Rocources, Inc.
Stamford, CT

MOORE
RESOURCES
McCORMACK

Baxter Healthcare Corporation
Deerfield, IL

Baxter Healthcare Corporation

Norfolk Southern Corporation
Norfolk, VA

NORFOLK
SOUTHERN

NYNEX Corporation
White Plains, NY

PPG Industries, Inc.
Pittsbugh, PA

Kellogg Company
Battle Creek, MI

Analog Devices
Norwood, MA

Reynolds Aluminum
Richmond, VA

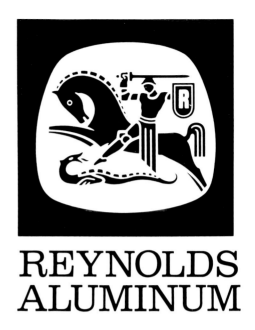

REYNOLDS
ALUMINUM

Millipore Corporation
Bedford, MA

MILLIPORE

Boise Cascade Corporation
Boise, ID

Boise Cascade
Corporation

Indiana National Corporation
Indianapolis, IN

Indiana National.
Pioneers in Banking.   Member FDIC

CoreStates Financial Corp.
Philadelphia, PA

CoreStates
Financial Corp

Arvin Industries, Inc.
Columbus, IN

Cummins Engine Company, Inc.
Columbus, IN

EMC Corporation
Hopkinton, MA

Mead
Dayton, OH

Medtronic, Inc.
Minneapolis, MN

Medtronic

The Dun & Bradstreet Corporation
New York, NY

DB The Dun & Bradstreet Corporation

Carpenter Technology Corporation
Reading, PA

CARPENTER TECHNOLOGY

CarTech

American President Companies, LTD.
Oakland, CA

AMERICAN PRESIDENT COMPANIES, LTD.

ENTEX
Houston, TX

FRUEHAUF Corporation
Detroit, MI

CPC International, Inc.
Englewood Cliffs, NJ

Weyerhaeuser Company
Tacoma, WA

Citizens Utilities Company
Stamford, CT

Wang Laboratories, Inc.
Lowell, MA

AT&T
New York, NY

NERCO, Incorporated
Portland, OR

Kemper Group
Long Grove, IL

Centex Corporation
Dallas, TX

The Cleveland Electric Illuminating Co.
Cleveland, OH

Home Beneficial Life Insurance Company
Richmond, VA

American Family Life Assurance
Columbus, GA

Squibb Corporation
Princeton, NJ

Ladd Furniture, Inc.
High Point, NC

AMFAC, Incorporated
San Francisco, CA

Alexander & Baldwin, Inc.
Honolulu, HI

OG&E Electric Service
Oklahoma City, OK

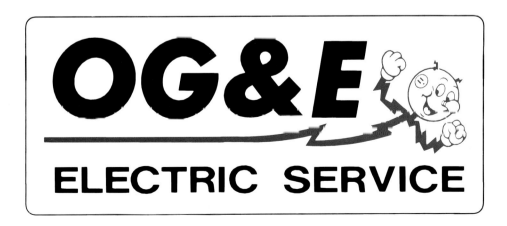

AM International
Chicago, IL

XEROX Corporation
Stamford, CT

XEROX®

Barnes Group, Inc.
Bristol, CT

162

Maxicare Health Plans, Inc.
Los Angeles, CA

Hershey
Hershey, PA

Hershey

Digital Communications Associates, Inc.
Alpharetta, GA

Oracle Corporation
Belmont, CA

ORACLE®

International Minerals
and Chemical Corporation
Northbrook, IL

KeyCorp
Albany, NY

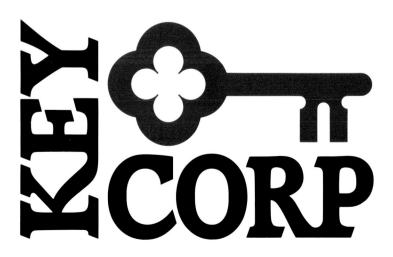

R.R. Donnelley & Sons Company
Chicago, IL

First Executive Corporation
Inglewood, CA

EXECUTIVE LIFE

American Water Works Service Co., Inc.
Haddon Heights, NJ

American
Water System

Nevada Power Company
Las Vegas, NV

Florida Progress Corporation
St. Petersburg, FL

CRAY Research, Inc.
Minneapolis, MN

SunTrust Banks, Inc.
Atlanta, GA

SUNTRUST

SunTrust Banks, Inc.
Atlanta, GA

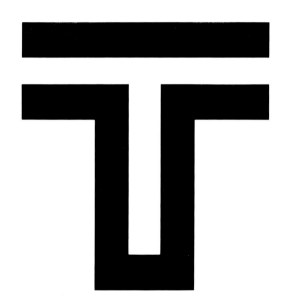

Trust Company Bank

CHEMED Corporation
Cincinnati, OH

CHEMED CORPORATION

Phillips Petroleum Company
Bartlesville, OK

Armorall Products Corporation
Irvin, CA

Kelly Services
Detroit, MI

AMAX Inc.
Greenwich, CT

U.S. BANCORP
Portland, OR

Morton Thiokol, Inc.
Chicago, IL

MORTON THIOKOL, INC.

Mercantile Bancorporation, Inc.
St. Louis, MO

Cyprus Minerals Company
Englewood, CO

Cyprus Minerals Company
Englewood, CO

CYPRUS

Texas Instruments
Dallas, TX

The Dow Chemical Co.
Midland, MI

Dayton Hudson Corp.
Minneapolis, MN

Diebold, Incorporated
Canton, OH

Aetna Life Insurance
Hartford, CT

Great American
Broadcasting Company
Cincinnati, OH

Bowne & Co., Inc.
New York, NY

The Coastal Corporation
Houston, TX

The Coastal Corporation

AMOCO Corporation
Chicago, IL

Eaton Corporation
Cleveland, OH

Table of Contents